·DEBATING·
IN THE MIDDLE GRADES

With 120 Debate Topics!

By Jim McAlpine, Betty Weincek, Sue Jeweler, & Marion Finkbinder
Illustrated by Karen Birchak

ISBN 978-1-56644-349-4
© 2009 Educational Impressions, Inc., Hawthorne, NJ

EDUCATIONAL IMPRESSIONS, INC.
Hawthorne, NJ 07507

Printed in the United States of America.

Table of Contents

TEACHER SECTION

AUDIENCE

- Grades 5-8
- All Ability Levels

- Whole Group
- Small Group

FOR

- Instruction
- Enrichment
- Extension
- Differentiation

GOALS/OBJECTIVES

- to explore debate as an activity and as a process

- to learn the components of debate and the debate process

- to encourage critical and analytical thinking

- to provide opportunities for higher-level thinking

- to improve public-speaking skills

- to integrate debate into the curriculum

- to encourage debating within the classroom and beyond

ABOUT THE BOOK

FORMAT

TEACHER SECTION

- Introduction
- Background
- Process for Teachers
- Simulation

STUDENT SECTION

- Introduction
- Background and Structure for Kids
- Vocabulary for Kids
- Process for Kids

DEBATE TOPICS

- Interdisciplinary
- Create Your Own

REFERENCES

MORE ABOUT THE BOOK

FLOW CHART

A flowchart is a graphic organizer that explains a step-by-step process. A flowchart that diagrams the sequence of the debate format used in this book is included.

VOCABULARY TERMS USED IN DEBATE

A selective list of words and phrases are included to help students learn and practice the process of debate.

THE DEBATE FORMAT/PROCESS

There are many different formats for debating. You may wish to research formats other than the one presented in this resource and give them a try.

DEBATE CHECKLIST

The Debate Checklist is a guide students may use to record their progress through the process as they follow the steps for participating in a debate. Students put a checkmark next to the tasks under each category and may also make notes in the margins. They should find the checklist helpful as they plan and prepare for the debate. The checklist and rubric are coordinated so that when students verify that they have done each task, their final evaluation should reflect their successful completion of the suggested steps within the debate process.

RUBRIC FOR DEBATE: OPTIONS

A rubric is a clear and concise explanation of the expectations for earning points or a grade for a student product. You may choose to use either of these rubrics as is, design your own, or create a new one with students. Students should agree to and be given the rubric prior to their debate in order to understand how their participation in the debate will be evaluated.

BE IT RESOLVED...!

A list of "issues"—matters that can have differing points of view, stands or sides—is provided. The list is divided into categories and reflects an interdisciplinary approach for topics from an array of disciplines. An interdisciplinary approach integrates thinking and learning skills and unifies both content and process. You may choose to use the issues provided, create your own based upon your curriculum, or use the student-made Create Your Own! activity issues.

INTRODUCTION

Kids debate issues all of the time. One can hear them in the classroom, on the playground, or in the lunch room and know that they take sides for or against issues at home, in the community and in other aspects and activities of their lives. Teaching children how to debate more effectively and efficiently as part of the school curriculum will give them essential skills in critical thinking, public speaking, and organization. It will also help them understand the importance of research. Language Arts and Social Studies National Standards can be addressed as an adjunct to the debate process, along with developing skills in the following areas:

- analytical thinking
- abstract thinking
- point of view
- persuasion techniques
- distinguishing between fact and opinion
- clarity
- ethics
- etiquette
- teamwork and cooperation

DEBATING IN THE MIDDLE GRADES is for students in grades 5–8. It is designed so that students can learn the debate process and procedures as well as how and when to apply these learned strategies to a variety of debate activities and formats. The goal is to ignite an interest in and fascination with debating for students so that they may use the skills in everyday situations and possibly in the future in curricular and extra-curricular activities and in their career choices.

What Is a Debate?

A debate is a discussion between people who have different points of view regarding a specific statement about an issue. The individuals in a debate speak either for or against an issue and state their case to an audience, which may include a judge or a panel of judges, who come to a decision about who won the debate. A statement, also known as a "motion" or a "proposition," is made so that the participants in the debate know exactly what specific aspect of an issue is to be debated. For example, a statement might be, "Kids should be able to use cell phones in school." There are steps to follow so that the arguments shared by both sides of the issue can be effective, efficient and fairly represented and presented.

KINDS OF DEBATES

INFORMAL DEBATE

An informal debate is a discussion between people who have two different points of view regarding a specific statement about an issue. It is not a contest and does not follow any other specific rules.

FORMAL DEBATE

A formal debate is a discussion between people who have two different points of view regarding a statement about a specific issue. This is a rule-based, competitive style of debate that requires a great deal of planning. Each side must follow specific steps. One side is in favor of the statement ("for" or "affirmative"), and the other side is opposed to the statement ("against" or "negative"). The debate is judged by a non-involved third party and a winner is determined based upon the effectiveness of the arguments given.

EXTEMPORANEOUS DEBATE

An extemporaneous debate is a discussion between people who have two different points of view regarding a specific statement about an issue. This type of debate does not allow the debaters to plan their arguments in advance. They are usually given research articles to read just before the debate so that they can use that information when making their arguments. The debaters have to "think on their feet." There is a procedure to follow, but it is more relaxed than in a formal debate.

PUBLIC DEBATE

A public debate is a discussion between two teams, each with two debaters, who are told which side to take when debating a specific point about a topic. Before they begin, the teams are given fifteen minutes to prepare an outline of their position and points to be made. There is little planning, but the debaters must have a lot of background knowledge and information about a variety of topics.

LINCOLN-DOUGLAS DEBATE FORMAT

This type of debate format is named for the Lincoln-Douglas debates which took place during the 1858 Illinois Senate race between Abraham Lincoln, a Republican, and Stephen A. Douglas, a Democrat. The Lincoln-Douglas debates of 1858 followed the following format: One of the two began by speaking on a self-chosen topic for an hour. The other candidate then spoke for an hour and a half to both offer a rebuttal and/or to introduce a topic of his own. The first speaker would then rebut for another half an hour. They alternated first and second positions throughout their series of meetings. The modern format involves two debaters who attempt to convince a judge of the acceptability of his or her side of a proposition. One debater argues the affirmative side and the other argues the negative side. The order of speakers, type of speech and minutes allotted are strictly regulated.

U.S. PRESIDENTIAL DEBATES

Debates are often held between or among candidates for the office of President of the Untied States. They debate their positions on any number of issues and topics. Televised versions have been part of the process since 1960. Topics for discussion are chosen by an individual or by a group of moderators without the prior knowledge of the debaters. Participants alternate giving timed responses to points raised by the moderator(s). No winner is formally determined at the time of the debate.

Other types of debates include Online Debate, Comedy Debate, Policy Debate, Classical Debate, and Public Forum debate.

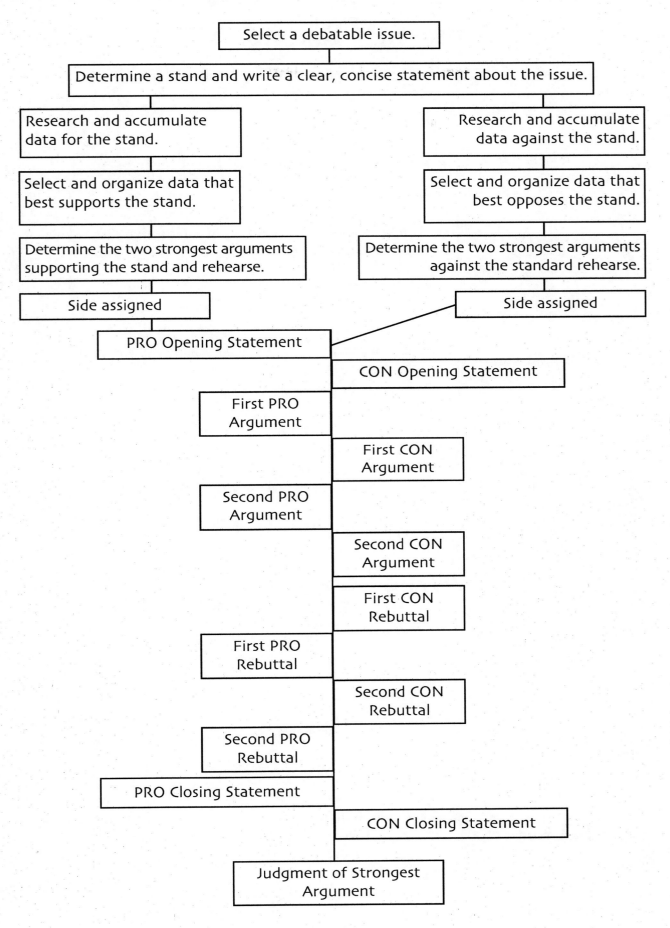

Select a debatable issue.

Determine a stand and write a clear, concise statement about the issue.

Research and accumulate data for the stand.

Research and accumulate data against the stand.

Select and organize data that best supports the stand.

Select and organize data that best opposes the stand.

Determine the two strongest arguments supporting the stand and rehearse.

Determine the two strongest arguments against the standard rehearse.

Side assigned

Side assigned

PRO Opening Statement

CON Opening Statement

First PRO Argument

First CON Argument

Second PRO Argument

Second CON Argument

First CON Rebuttal

First PRO Rebuttal

Second CON Rebuttal

Second PRO Rebuttal

PRO Closing Statement

CON Closing Statement

Judgment of Strongest Argument

Bloom's Taxonomy

The debate activities provide opportunities for students to experience and practice the levels of Bloom's Taxonomy.

Bloom's Taxonomy is a theory ordering the levels of the thinking process.

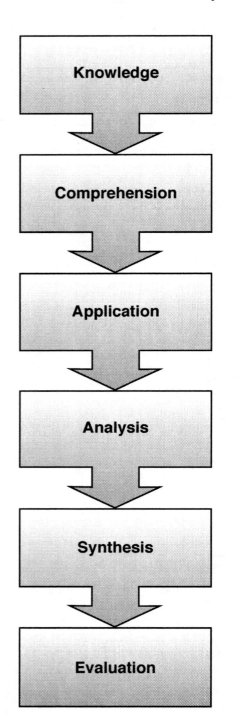

Knowledge is the recalling of information that is known. (What do you know?)

Comprehension is the understanding of the information. (What does the information mean?)

Application is using/applying the information to a new situation. (How can you use what you know and understand?)

Analysis is dissecting information into its component parts. (How does what you know and understand work?)

Synthesis is creating a "whole" from parts of existing information. (How can you make something new from what you know and understand?)

Evaluation is assessing the value of material based on established criteria. (Is what you created effective and efficient?)

Creative Problem Solving

Creative Problem Solving (CPS) is a way to solve problems, step by step, until you reach a solution.

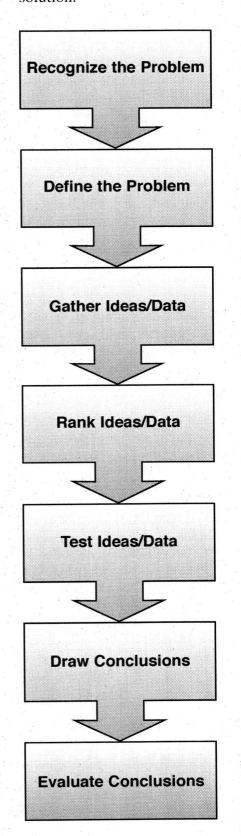

Recognize the Problem is realizing that there is a situation that requires a solution. (Does a problem exist?)

Define the Problem is stating the problem situation in your own words. (What needs to be solved?)

Gather Ideas/Data is brainstorming/collecting/finding ideas/data related to the problem. (What is known about the problem? What more do I need to find out? Where do I find out?)

Rank Ideas/Data is organizing the gathered information into a logical order that is most feasible for solving the problem. (What makes the most sense for solving the problem?)

Test Ideas/Data is using the ranked ideas to see which ones produce a solution to the problem. (Which ideas work?)

Draw Conclusions is examining the solutions to determine which seem to be best. (Which solution will become the response to the problem?)

Evaluate Conclusions is examining the solution for its effectiveness and efficiency in solving the problem. (Does the response solve the problem?)

Research Scheme

Research is a sequential, hierarchical process for discovering and organizing principles or facts about a given subject.

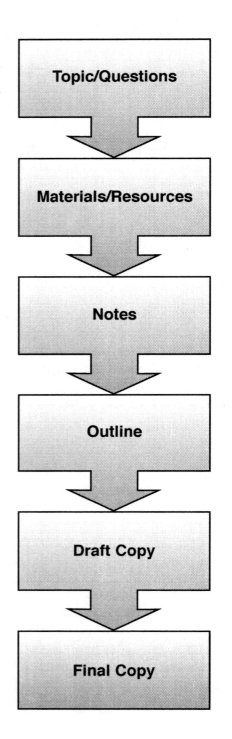

The **Topic** is the subject to be researched. It may be assigned or chosen. **Questions** are queries—assigned or self-selected—related to the **Topic**. (What is the thesis statement?)

The **Materials/Resources** are the sources of information to be used in researching the topic/questions. (What data do I need and where can I find it?)

Notes are important pieces of information concerning the topic/questions taken from the materials/resources and recorded for later use. (What information do I need to record?)

The **Outline** is a way to structure and organize the information accumulated in the **Notes**. (How do I order the recorded information?)

The **Draft** is a preliminary narrative compilation of information related to the topic/questions developed from the outline. (How might I present the preliminary response to the thesis statement?)

The **Final Copy** is the product which is a response to the topic/questions posed. (Does the outcome effectively/efficiently address the thesis statement?)

Scientific Method

The Scientific Method is one documented procedure for performing an investigation that allows others to follow the same steps to verify or refute conclusions. It includes five hierarchal steps:

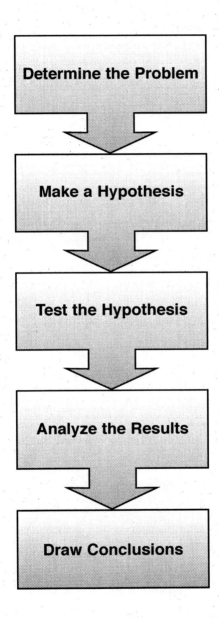

Determine the Problem

Make a Hypothesis

Test the Hypothesis

Analyze the Results

Draw Conclusions

INTEGRATION OF DEBATE, BLOOM'S TAXONOMY, CPS, RESEARCH SCHEME, & SCIENTIFIC METHOD

DEBATE	BLOOM'S TAXONOMY	CREATIVE PROBLEM SOLVING	RESEARCH SCHEMA	SCIENTIFIC METHOD
SELECT A DEBATABLE ISSUE Select or be assigned a broad, general topic for which there can be a pro and a con.	KNOWLEDGE That which is known	RECOGNIZE THE PROBLEM Realize that there is an unresolved situation.	TOPIC/ QUESTIONS What is to be found out	DETERMINE THE PROBLEM Identify the unknown or what is to be proven.
IDENTIFY A CLEAR, CONCISE STATEMENT ABOUT THE ISSUE. DETERMINE A STAND RE: THE ISSUE STATEMENT Within the general topic, determine the specific, concise sub-topic that is to be debated, pro and con.	KNOWLEDGE/ COMPREHENSION That which is known and understood	DEFINE THE PROBLEM State clearly what needs to be resolved.	TOPIC/ QUESTIONS Focusing on a specific thesis	DETERMINE THE PROBLEM Identify and limit the problem to be solved to the most specific level possible.
RESEARCH AND ACCUMU-LATE DATA APPROPRIATE TO SUPPORT THE STAND Assemble factual, relevant supportable information to back-up one or both sides on the issue/topic.	KNOWLEDGE/ COMPREHENSION/ APPLICATION That which is known, understood and can be utilized	GATHER IDEAS/DATA Obtain as much information as possible related to the unresolved situation.	MATERIALS/ RESOURCES/ NOTES Locating a broad spectrum of information	HYPOTHESIZE Create an estimated or anticipated result of the procedure.

DEBATE	BLOOM'S TAXONOMY	CREATIVE PROBLEM SOLVING	RESEARCH SCHEMA	SCIENTIFIC METHOD
SELECT AND ORGANIZE BEST SUPPORTING DATA. KEEP ALL DATA FOR REBUTTAL Cull through collected information/data to identify best for both sides of the issue.	APPLICATION/ ANALYSIS That which is known, understood and can be utilized while appreciating background and extensions	RANK IDEAS/DATA Organize the information into usability for resolving the situation.	NOTES/ OUTLINE Sort data for most relevancy and create rough, product outline.	HYPOTHESIZE Identify and limit the estimated or anticipated result of the procedure the most specific level possible.
DETERMINE TWO STRONGEST ARGUMENTS TO SUPPORT POSITION. PRACTICE PRESENTATION After determining side on the issue, create and rehearse pro or con statements and/or rebuttals.	ANALYSIS/ SYNTHESIS That which is known, understood and can be utilized in usual and unusual ways while appreciating background and extensions	TEST IDEAS/DATA Determine which ideas for resolving the situation are most likely to work.	OUTLINE/ DRAFT Restructure out-line as needed and proceed to content draft(s).	TEST THE HYPOTHESIS Proceed with trials of the possible solutions or proof for the problem/ hypothesis.

DEBATE	BLOOM'S TAXONOMY	CREATIVE PROBLEM SOLVING	RESEARCH SCHEMA	SCIENTIFIC METHOD
PROCEED THROUGH FORMAL DEBATE PROCESS Pro opening statement Con opening statement First pro argument First con argument Second pro argument Second con argument First con rebuttal First pro rebuttal Second con rebuttal Second pro rebuttal Pro closing statement Con closing statement	ANALYSIS/ SYNTHESIS/ EVALUATION Assessing the worth or value of that which is known, understood and can be utilized in usual and unusual ways while appreciating background and extensions	DRAW CONCLUSIONS Decide which of the ideas will be the approach to resolving the situation.	DRAFT Edit and finalize content draft and proceed to proofing draft.	ANALYZE THE RESULTS Determine the viability of the trials as each relates to possible proof or solution to the hypothesis.
JUDGES DETERMINE THE SIDE MAKING THE STRONGEST ARGUMENT Non-involved third party (parties) assesses winner using pre-determined grading rubric.	SYNTHESIS/ EVALUATION Assessment of the new or unusual ways to use data or materials	EVALUATE CONCLUSIONS Decide if the proposed solution actually resolves the problem.	FINAL DOCUMENT Submit edited and proofed product for assessment.	DRAW CONCLUSIONS Determine the validity of the hypothesis based on the results of the trials used to solve or prove it.

Interdisciplinary Approach

Interdisciplinary is defined as a concept view and curriculum approach that deliberately applies a variety of methodology and language from an array of discipline fields to examine a theme, problem, issue, experience or topic. An interdisciplinary approach integrates thinking and learning skills and unifies content and process. Students get a range of stimulating and motivating curriculum experiences that engage them in thoughtful confrontation with subject matter while fostering abstract thinking.

An interdisciplinary theme can be followed through science and/or language arts, mathematics, social studies and/or the arts. In schools with departments and/or grade-level teams, teachers can work together to help students link knowledge and make connections between and across content areas. Interdisciplinary instruction allows for flexibility and can help make concepts and content relevant for students.

Differentiation can be addressed through an interdisciplinary approach. A variety of student interest and strengths can be targeted. The materials and resources used by teachers and students for the activities can be chosen for their appropriate instructional or interest level. Evaluations of student responses to the activities should reflect the cognitive and creative ability of the students. They many range from concrete to the more abstract operations.

Differentiation

Differentiation is a way of thinking about instruction and planning in order to meet the diverse needs of students based on their unique characteristics. Instruction is differentiated in three ways: through the content, the process and/or the product of a program objective or unit of study.

Content may be differentiated through acceleration, enrichment or extension. In order to provide different or extended opportunities for students, time must be provided. One way to do this is through compacting, which includes pre-assessment of objectives and the telescoping of some instruction so that students may master needed information more quickly and perhaps independently. An interdisciplinary approach to instruction is another form of content differentiation.

Process, or the internalization of information, may be differentiated through increasing time spent on complex thinking skills. The students' involvement in their own learning is key to process differentiation. Students are encouraged to select some of the activities in which they will be engaged productively and to evaluate their own and/or their peers' work based on some self-selected and teacher-approved criteria.

Product differentiation is the outcome of the application of the processes to the content. Variety is encouraged. The product—whether verbal, active or visual—should be accurate, organized and coherent. Self-evaluation is a key element in production. Real products for real audiences are encouraged.

Tiered assignments allow teachers to assign different groups of students within the same lesson or unit. The following guidelines can increase effectiveness:

- Focus the assignment on a key concept.
- Use a variety of materials at different levels of complexity.
- Adjust the assignment by complexity, level of abstraction, number of steps and degree of student independence.
- At each level, establish clear expectations and provide specific criteria for achieving excellence.

Suggestions

AS YOU USE THIS BOOK WITH STUDENTS, YOU MAY CHOOSE TO...

- introduce the descriptions of various types of debates to provide background information;

- use all or selected debate activity sheets with students;

- differentiate instruction by choosing debate activities appropriate for individual students, small groups, or whole-group instruction;

- have students keep a glossary of the debate terms and explanations in their notebooks as a reference;

- use the debate materials as a unit of study or throughout the school year in a variety of content areas;

- design and implement a formal debate/forensic competition in your class, with other classes, or throughout the school;

- create/sponsor a Debate Club; and/or

- have students develop and implement new or different use/application ideas for debate.

SIMULATION

A simulation is a representation of a real process. This simulation is designed to act as an example for debating in the middle grades. Components for this debate simulation include the following:

- Debate topic

- Key words/phrases for research

- An example of gathered research

- Graphic organizers that may aid students as they utilize the research to prepare their debate

You may choose to use the simulation in the following ways:

- A guide for understanding the debate process

- An instructional example

- A model for an actual debate topic that you can use with your class

- A hand-out to be used by students in preparation for their own debate experience

BE IT RESOLVED...

Debate Topic:
Tiddlywinks must be an Olympic event.

RESEARCH

SEARCH TOPICS (KEY WORDS/PHRASES)

TIDDLYWINKS	OLYMPICS
Tiddlywinks	Olympics
Tiddlywinks Origins	Olympics Definition
Tiddlywinks History	Definition of Sports/Games
Tiddlywinks Rules	Olympics Events
Tiddlywinks Associations/Organizations	Olympics Eligibility Criteria for Selection
Tiddlywinks Local/Global	Olympics Charter
	IOC

Tiddlywinks

- The original game was an adult craze in England, the United States and Europe throughout the 1890s.

- Tournament tiddlywinks requires both strategy and manual skill.

- It was organized at Cambridge University in England.

- This game differs greatly from the children's game of tiddlywinks. The children's game involves merely flicking the winks into a cup.

- How to Play: Winks normally is played by four people, each winker controlling one of the colors—blue, green, red, or yellow. In singles games one player controls both colors of a partnership (red and blue play against green and yellow). Each color has six winks, two large and four small. Winks are played by pressing or flicking them with a squidger, a larger plastic disc one to two inches in diameter. The game, whether four players or singles, is played on a 3 foot by 6 foot felt mat. A time limit of 25 minutes is used (20 for Singles) for the first round, after which five additional rounds are played if a potout (the achievement of having all winks of a color in the pot) has not occurred.

- Support from Prince Philip.

- Support from Guinness.

- Since North American Tiddlywinks Association (1955), there have been more than 200 official tournaments, over 9,000 tournament games, and more than 600 winkers.

- Celebrations of the 50th anniversary in 2005 brought winkers from around the globe to the United States.

The Olympics

- The Olympic Games is an international multi-sport event.

- Currently, the Olympic program consists of 35 different sports, 53 disciplines and more than 400 events.

- The IOC reviews the Olympic program at the first Session following each Olympiad. A simple majority is required for an Olympic sport to be included in the Olympic program. Under the current rules, an Olympic sport not selected for inclusion in a particular Games remains an Olympic sport and may be included again later with a simple majority.

- Until 1992, the Olympics also often featured demonstration sports. The objective was for these sports to reach a larger audience; the winners of these events are not official Olympic champions. These sports were sometimes sports popular only in the host nation; however, internationally known sports have also been demonstrated. Some of these demonstration sports eventually were included as full-medal events.

- A sport's statutes, practice and activities must conform with the Olympic Charter.

  "Olympism is a philosophy of life, exalting and combining in a balanced whole the qualities of body, will and mind. Blending sport with culture and education, Olympism seeks to create a way of life based on the joy found in effort, the educational value of good example and respect for universal fundamental ethical principles."

- In order to promote the Olympic Movement, the IOC can recognize any international non-governmental organization that administers one or more sports at world level and encompassing organizations administering such sports at a national level as an International Sports Federation.

- Any sport is eligible to become a medal sport as long as it can be scored and meets certain criteria.

  The first step to becoming a recognized sport of the Summer Games requires being organized into an international federation that can apply on behalf of the sport. Someone must fill in the application.

  A sport must also be popular in many countries. Each federation must have male participants in at least 75 countries on four continents and female participants in at least 40 countries on three continents. The first step to becoming a recognized sport of the Winter Games requires being organized into an international federation and having participants in at least 25 countries for winter sports.

  The potential Olympic sport must support ranked events. Any event which competes as an Olympic sport or competes within one of its disciplines will provide scores, timing or another method of measuring competitors. These measures will result in a ranking at the end of the event and will lead to the award of medals, ribbons, certificates or other non-monetary recognition of the rank earned.

The events must hold competitions on a world level. To be included in the Olympic Program, an event must be recognized internationally in both participant numbers and geographically. An event is required to have been featured at least twice in either world or continental championships.

Physical, not mechanical, athletic performance is required. Sports, disciplines or events in which performance depends essentially on mechanical propulsion are not acceptable.

• Organized and consistent lobbying is needed to help promote selection over other sports. This should be done without bribery, which is banned from Olympic sports promotional activity.

• A prospective Olympic sport will sometimes make its first appearance as a demonstration, or non-medal winning sport, before becoming an official Olympic sport. There are three ways an activity can come into the Olympics:

as a completely new sport and federation as described above;

as a new discipline that is a branch of an existing Olympic sport; or

as a new event that is a competition within an existing discipline.

• The admission or exclusion of a sport falls within the jurisdiction of the IOC Session of the IOC Executive Board. The International Olympic Committee process requires seven years for a new sport to be added.

YES and NO!
(FOR OR AGAINST)
Part 1

Record the data you have accumulated from your research regarding both sides the debate topic prior to knowing which side of issue will be your responsibility.

DEBATE TOPIC:
Tiddlywinks must be an Olympic event.

YES (FOR)	NO (AGAINST)
Tournament Tiddlywinks requires both strategy and manual skill.	Child's game
Support from Prince Philip	Support only because it is a novelty
Support from Guinness	Guinness supports all kinds of weirdness
More than 200 official tournaments, over 9000 tournament games, and more than 600 winkers	Primarily in United States and England
Winkers from around the globe	Few in the wider world.
Tiddlywinks conforms with the Olympic Charter.	
Any sport is eligible to become a medal sport as long as it can be scored and meets certain criteria: an international federation that can apply on behalf of the sport (someone to fill in the application); must be popular in many countries; must support ranked events; must hold competitions on a world level; and must require physical and not mechanical athletic performance.	There is no international federation; it is not in many countries (does not have male participants in at least 75 countries on 4 continents and female participants in at least 40 countries on 3 continents); has not been featured at least twice in world or continental championships. It is not a branch of an existing Olympic sport; it is not within an existing discipline.

YES and NO!
(FOR OR AGAINST)
Part 2

Based on all of your research, choose and record the strongest arguments supporting each stand on the issue. Refer to your research data base as needed.

DEBATE TOPIC:
Tiddlywinks must be an Olympic event.

YES (FOR)	NO (AGAINST)
Tiddlywinks requires both strategy and manual skill.	Child's game.
Tiddlywinks conforms with the Olympic Charter.	
Any sport is eligible to become a medal sport as long as it can be scored and meets certain criteria: an international federation that can apply on behalf of the sport (someone to fill in the application); must be popular in many countries; must support ranked events; must hold competitions on a world level; and must require physical and not mechanical athletic performance.	There is no international federation; it is not in many countries (does not have male participants in at least 75 countries on 4 continents and female participants in at least 40 countries on 3 continents); has not been featured at least twice in world or continental championships.
	It is not a branch of an existing Olympic sport; it is not within an existing discipline.

YES and NO!
(FOR OR AGAINST)
Part 3

**Here are two options, the choice of which should be made
PRIOR to selecting an issue to debate!**

1. The moderator can randomly assign
a side for the issue. This means that
you should be equally prepared
to take either point of view
on the issue.

2. The opposing teams or individual
participants may have pre-selected their
stand and agreed on their positions
regarding the issue at hand.
This method allows for more directed
and focused preparation,
especially for those new to
the debating process.

YES and NO!
(FOR OR AGAINST)
Part 4

YES - FOR

Determine the two strongest arguments for your position on the issue and rehearse in preparation for the debate. Information from the FOR and AGAINST sides of the issue may be useful as negations for the opposite point of view.

DEBATE TOPIC:
Tiddlywinks must be an Olympic event.

ARGUMENT #1

Tiddlywinks fulfills the Olympic credo from its Charter. It balances body, will, and mind and combines sports, science, and the joy of participation.

ARGUMENT #2

Tiddlywinks, like all Olympic sports, requires practice, skill, and tenacity. This results in an easily understandable and doable scoring format.

YES and NO!
(FOR OR AGAINST)
Part 4

NO - AGAINST

Determine the two strongest arguments for your position on the issue and rehearse in preparation for the debate. Information from the FOR and AGAINST sides of the issue may be useful as negations for the opposite point of view.

DEBATE TOPIC:

Tiddlywinks must be an Olympic event.

ARGUMENT #1

Tiddlywinks is not a real Olympic sport because it does not comply with the 10 criteria for entry. It does not play in the required 72 countries.

ARGUMENT #2

Tiddlywinks does not appear as an offshoot or permutation of any known Olympic sport—if, in fact, it is a sport.

MY PLANNING SHEETS
YES -FOR

You know the debatable issue, have completed your research, have determined the strongest arguments, and have been assigned to or selected a specific stand. Now it is time to get ready for the debate. Use the following pages to plan and prepare what you will say during the debate. Remember to use the DEBATE CHECKLIST!

OPENING STATEMENT
Tiddlywinks must be an Olympic sport.

FIRST ARGUMENT
Tiddlywinks fulfills the Olympic credo from its Charter. Tiddlywinks balances body, will, and mind and combines sports, science, and the joy of participation.

SECOND ARGUMENT
Tiddlywinks, like all Olympic sports, requires practice, skill, and tenacity. This results in an easily understandable and doable scoring format.

FIRST REBUTTAL: Based on the Opposition's Argument(s)
Sports like snowboarding, wind surfing, dressage, and the pentathlon are not played in 72 countries.

SECOND REBUTTAL: Based on the Opposition's Argument(s)
Basketball, soccer, and dressage are not offshoots or a permutation of an Olympic sport.

CLOSING STATEMENT: Making the Strongest Possible Summation Supporting Your Position on the Issue
Tiddlywinks fulfills the Olympic credo from its Charter and balances body, will, and mind and combines sports, science, and the joy of participation. Tiddlywinks, like all Olympic sports, requires practice, skill, and tenacity. Other Olympic sports do not completely follow either the Charter or guidelines and have been played in Olympics around the world for many years. Therefore, Tiddlywinks must be an Olympic sport.

MY PLANNING SHEETS
NO -AGAINST

You know the debatable issue, have completed your research, have determined the strongest arguments, and have been assigned to or selected a specific stand. Now it is time to get ready for the debate. Use the following pages to plan and prepare what you will say during the debate. Remember to use the DEBATE CHECKLIST!

OPENING STATEMENT

Tiddlywinks must not be an Olympic sport.

FIRST ARGUMENT

Tiddlywinks is not a real Olympic sport because it does not comply with the 10 criteria for entry. It does not play in the required 72 countries.

SECOND ARGUMENT

Tiddlywinks does not appear as an offshoot or permutation on any known Olympic sport, if in fact, it is a sport.

FIRST REBUTTAL: Based on the Opposition's Argument(s)

Tiddlywinks is simply a child's game; it is not a sport.

SECOND REBUTTAL: Based on the Opposition's Argument(s)

Tiddlywinks is a toy-based game rather than a sport.

CLOSING STATEMENT: Making the Strongest Possible Summation Supporting Your Position on the Issue

Tiddlywinks is a child's game—a toy. The 10 criteria are very clearly stated for entry into the Olympics, and Tiddlywinks does not comply. It is not played in the required 72 countries. It does not have male participants in at least 75 countries on 4 continents and female participants in at least 40 countries on 3 continents. Tiddlywinks does not appear as an offshoot or permutation on any known Olympic sport. Therefore, Tiddlywinks must not be an Olympic event.

STUDENT SECTION

Introduction

Have you ever been in a discussion with another person in which each of you represented a different side of the same issue? Maybe you disagreed about how much homework is too much or whether one political candidate is better qualified. You might have argued about the impact of violence on TV or whether there is an alternative for war. Perhaps you disagreed on the value of hip-hop music. Your discussion or argument involving opposing points of view on some issue was, in fact, an informal debate. If the question you discussed was a contest of argumentation in which two opposing teams or individuals would defend and attack a proposition or statement, you would have been involved in a more structured, formal debate.

Debating has been around for a very long time. The early Greeks are given credit for creating a kind of democratic government with rule by representatives elected by the male landowners. These elected representatives made important political and social decisions for the whole city-state. The Greeks, as a result of this dynamic form of governing, developed the art and skill of public speaking and debate so that important elections and issues could be openly analyzed. Isocrates, born in 436 BCE, was one of the first teachers of public speaking. Other great speakers were Socrates and Demosthenes, both of whom were and are known for their great speeches. Romans who influenced debating and speaking include Marcus Tullius Cicero (106-43 BCE), the author of "De Oratore," which included a discussion of opposing views held by opposing characters, and Marcus Fabius Quintillian, born in 43 CE, who wrote a work on public speaking designed as a training manual for politicians and lawyers. It was used until the twentieth century. Debating has had roles in politics, economics, conflicts, and diplomacy throughout history.

Why is debate an important skill to learn and practice? How does a debate work? What are the components? What are the steps to follow for a formal debate? These questions will be explored through a collection of fun and dynamic activities so that you will become a "great debater"!

Why Learn the Skill of Debating?

Debating is an important skill to learn and practice. Learning how to debate will give you important skills in critical thinking, public speaking, organization, and recognizing the importance of research. When you participate in a debate you will…

- use analytical thinking
     to be able to separate ideas and study what they mean

- use abstract thinking
     to use concepts and to make and understand ideas

- understand point of view
     to comprehend a position from which something is observed or considered

- use persuasion techniques
     to use strategies to win someone over, as by reasoning or personal forcefulness

- understand the difference between fact and opinion
     to distinguish between a true statement and a personal belief or judgment

- practice clarity
     to use clearness of thought or style

- understand ethics
     to know a set of principles of right conduct

- practice etiquette
     to use manners

- practice teamwork and cooperation
     to work together toward a common end or purpose

When you learn this debate process and procedure, you will know how and when to apply these learned strategies to a variety of debate activities and formats. The goal is to ignite your interest in and fascination with debating so that you may use these skills in everyday situations and could possibly use them all through your years in school, in your extra-curricular activities, and even in your career choices.

Vocabulary

The following list of words and phrases will help you as you learn and practice the process of debate.

affirmative   a stand in favor of or support of an issue

annotated bibliography   citation of sources accompanied by explanatory notes for each

appealing   quality of being attractive

argument   a reasonable stand intended to persuade for or against

closing statement   a summation of significant argument points meant to persuade the judge(s) to side with a particular stand on the issue

concise   brief and to the point; the quality of being without elaboration or detail

controlled   regulated and abiding by rules and boundaries

courtesy   mannerly consideration and cooperation

credible   supportably believable

criteria   established standards, rules or expectations

debate   a controlled discussion of an issue with the presentations and rebuttals of opposing stands

decorum   orderliness and politeness

dignity   the quality of being worthy of respect or honor; formal reserve or seriousness of manner

emphasis   intensity of expression or stress that gives importance to something

etiquette   rules that guide socially acceptable and appropriate behavior

extemporaneous   composed or uttered without planning; used to describe an unplanned discussion in a debate between participants, usually in the rebuttal/response portion

formal debate	a contest of argumentation in which two opposing teams or individuals present their stand, attack the opposing stand and then defend their stand regarding a proposition or statement
format	a plan of organization and execution
goal	an end toward which one's efforts are aimed
inflection	a change in tone or loudness of voice
informal debate	an open discussion or argument involving opposing points of view on some issue
intonation	a change in pitch of voice
issue	a controversial matter that can inspire differing points of view, stands or sides
judge	a person(s) whose job is to record arguments, rebuttals, and supports to determine the winning side in a debate
moderator	a person responsible for maintaining debate protocol
negative	having the quality of being opposed to an issue
opening statement	a persuasive, supported, and emotional presentation to the opposing side and the audience by each side of the debated issue
opinion	a belief
persuasive	intended to change others' opinions or beliefs or to incite to action
point of order	a question challenging whether the debate protocol is being followed
primary source	supportive data coming from original materials, direct observation, or first-person knowledge
proposition	the point to be discussed or maintained in an argument as stated in sentence form near the start
protocol	a detailed, pre-determined debate procedure

question	what the debate is seeking to resolve, including the issue and two opposing stands regarding the issue
rebuttal	a substantive response to a point supporting a stand that weakens the strength of that stand
relevant	appropriate; tending to prove or disprove an issue under discussion
research	collection of information about the debate topic
role	the job performed in a debate
round	one argument with supports or rebuttals from each side of the issue
ruling	a decision made by a moderator or judge in a debate
side or stand	a position or attitude on an issue or a specific statement about an issue
speech	oral communication of thoughts through speaking
summary	a review of the main points
support	a point to uphold an argument
tally	the record of scores earned
validity	the quality of having relevance and logic

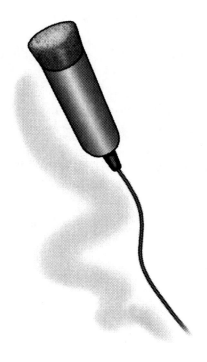

A Formal Debate

There are many different formats for debating. After you learn the components and practice the steps listed here, you and your teacher may wish to research other formats and give them a try!

STEPS TO FOLLOW FOR A FORMAL DEBATE:

1. SELECT A DEBATABLE ISSUE
The issue may be pre-selected by the moderator or by the participants or may be selected randomly at the start of preparation.

2. DETERMINE A STAND
The stands taken by the participants may be assigned by the moderator, randomly selected, or pre-determined by the participants.

3. RESEARCH AND ACCUMULATE DATA
Participants must locate relevant, supportable, factual data to justify their pro or con stand on the issue.

4. SELECT AND ORGANIZE
Participants must prioritize the information located and rank the information from most important and useable to the least.

5. DETERMINE THE TWO STRONGEST
Participants must identify, formulate and practice the strongest statements possible supporting their position on the issue.

6. SIDE ASSIGNED
Assigning a side is usually reserved for more advanced debaters and is done by the moderator.

7. "PRO" OPENING STATEMENT
The debater supporting the issue makes the most significant and substantive argument possible for his or her stand.

8. "CON" OPENING STATEMENT
The debater opposing the issue makes the most significant and substantive argument possible for his or her stand.

9. FIRST "PRO" ARGUMENT
The debater supporting the issue expands his or her position using supportive data gathered in research.

10. FIRST "CON" ARGUMENT
The debater opposing the issue expands his or her position using supportive data gathered in research.

11. SECOND "PRO" ARGUMENT

The debater supporting the issue further expands his or her position using supportive data gathered in research.

12. SECOND "CON" ARGUMENT

The debater opposing the issue further expands his or her position using supportive data gathered in research.

13. FIRST "CON" REBUTTAL

The debater opposing the issue presents a civilized disagreement in which points are made and supported to refute or contradict the points made by the PRO arguments and statements.

14. FIRST "PRO" REBUTTAL

The debater supporting the issue presents a civilized disagreement in which points are made and supported to refute or contradict the points made by the CON arguments and statements.

15. SECOND "CON" REBUTTAL

The debater opposing the issue presents a civilized disagreement in which additional points are made and supported to refute or contradict the points made by the PRO arguments and statements.

16. SECOND "PRO" REBUTTAL

The debater supporting the issue presents a civilized disagreement in which additional points are made and supported to refute or contradict the points made by the CON arguments and statements.

17. "PRO" CLOSING STATEMENT

The debater supporting the issue is given the opportunity to summarize and justify the rationale for PRO position on the issue.

18. "CON" CLOSING STATEMENT

The debater opposing the issue is given the opportunity to summarize and justify the rationale for CON position on the issue.

19. JUDGMENT/EVALUATION

Based on the debaters' performance, use of supporting data and accuracy, a winner is determined.

Characteristics of a Good Debater

We are reminded to use manners every day. For example, we say, "Please" when we want something and "Thank you" when something is done for us. Manners are accepted, correct behaviors for any given social situation. *Etiquette* is defined as the rules that guide socially acceptable behavior. When engaging in a debate, there are rules—debate etiquette—which good debaters must follow.

A good debater should...

- be respectful to all participants in the debate;
- be prepared;
- make eye contact with his or her opponent, the audience and the judge(s) when speaking;
- stand still and in one place when speaking;
- be truthful and use facts to support his or her side;
- be polite and civil;
- remain calm and refrain from yelling and insulting his or her opponent;
- listen and not interrupt the another speaker(s); and
- congratulate his or her opponent at the end for a good debate.

Debate Checklist

Your debate will be judged and a winner will be determined. As you plan and prepare for your debate, use the following checklist. When you can put a checkmark next to the tasks under each category, you are on your way to a successful debate!

PRE-DEBATE:

Organization:

1. Know my role in the debate.   _____
2. Prepare carefully.   _____
3. Organize my notes/outline/cards.   _____
4. Write logical and concise arguments.   _____
5. Rank arguments according to effectiveness.   _____
6. Practice arguments.   _____
7. Time arguments.   _____
8. Take notes carefully for rebuttal.   _____

Research:

1. Define the issue and stand.   _____
2. Gather materials and resources.   _____
3. Take notes; make an outline to organize ideas.   _____
4. Record sources; prepare bibliography.   _____

DEBATE:

Procedure:

1. Use the correct debate format: _____
   - Submit the order of speakers to the judge before the debate begins. _____
   - Opening statement _____
   - Constructive speeches: _____
     - First affirmative _____
     - First negative _____
     - Second affirmative _____
     - Second negative _____
   - Rebuttal speeches: _____
     - First negative _____
     - First affirmative _____
     - Second negative _____
     - Second affirmative _____
   - Closing statement _____
2. Follow the rules of debate: _____
   - Affirmative side goes first.
   - One person speaks at a time. _____
   - Speaker presents one argument. _____
   - Speaker responds to one argument from the opposing side. _____

Presentation:

1. Make eye contact with the audience or judge when speaking. _____
2. Stand in one place when speaking. _____
3. Speak in a loud and clear voice. _____
4. Speak with inflection. _____
5. Listen and do not interrupt another speaker. _____
6. Dress appropriately. _____

Etiquette:

1. Be respectful to all participants in the debate. _____
2. Be polite. _____
3. Stay calm and refrain from yelling or making insulting remarks. _____
4. Accept the ruling of the judge. _____
5. Congratulate your opponent for a good debate. _____

Rubric for Debate

A rubric is a clear and concise explanation of the criteria, or expectations, for earning points or a grade for a product. Use this rubric before your debate in order to understand how your debate will be evaluated.

OPTIONS:

The judge(s) for a debate can use any means or method agreed upon by all the participants to determine the outcome of a debate. Offered here are two possible options. Holistic and Specific-Criteria Assessment.

Holistic

The judge(s) determines the winner(s) by utilizing an overall, subjective, impression assessment, possibly utilizing the following four basic levels of success:

- The debater demonstrates an effective, well-developed point of view that persuades and/or rebuts as intended.

- The debater demonstrates a somewhat-developed point of view that persuades and/or rebuts to some degree.

- The debater demonstrates an incomplete or oversimplified point of view that does not persuade and/or rebut as intended.

- The debater demonstrates an incomplete or oversimplified point of view that neither persuades nor rebuts as intended.

Specific Criteria Assessment

The judge(s) determines the "winner(s)" by utilizing a listing of specific criteria for each level of success. The "winner(s)" would, therefore, have met the greatest number of those criteria.

4-POINT AWARD

The debater demonstrated an effective, well-developed point of view that persuaded and/or rebuted as intended:

- Effectively and efficiently used his or her role in the debate

- Gathered and used researched and verifiable materials and resources

- Recorded sources in a bibliography

- Organized notes in an effective and efficient manner

- Effectively and efficiently defined his or her stand on the issue

- Presented logical, concise and well-supported arguments

- Presented arguments according to effectiveness

- Effectively rebutted the opposing view

- Used the correct debate format

3-POINT AWARD

The debater demonstrated a somewhat-developed point of view that did not persuade and/or rebut somewhat as intended:

- Followed his/her role in the debate

- Gathered and used materials and resources were somewhat verified

- Recorded sources in a bibliography

- Organized notes were available and used

- Defined the issue and his or her stand on it

- Presented arguments

- Presented arguments somewhat randomly

- Presented an acceptable rebuttal

- Used the correct debate format

2-POINT AWARD

The debater demonstrated an incomplete or oversimplified point of view that did not persuade and/or rebut as intended:

- Usually followed his or her role in the debate

- Gathered some materials and resources, but more were needed

- Recorded sources

- Notes poorly organized or absent

- Defined the issue and his or her stand on it ineffectively

- Presented arguments ineffectively

- Presented arguments with little apparent purpose or structure

- Presented a weak or ineffectual rebuttal

- Used the correct debate format at times

1-POINT AWARD

The debater demonstrated a little knowledge of the assignment and attempted to persuade and/or rebut:

- Demonstrated little knowledge of his or her role in the debate

- Gathered no or few materials and resources

- Had no record of sources used

- Had no notes

- Had no arguments or had poor arguments

- Had little or no structure to presentations or thinking behind them

- Made a poor rebuttal or had no rebuttal

- Used incorrect debate format

READY TO START!

SELECT A DEBATABLE ISSUE
The issue may be pre-selected by the moderator or by the participants or may be selected randomly at the start of preparation.

DETERMINE A STAND
The stands taken by the participants may be assigned by the moderator, randomly selected, or pre-determined by the participants.

RESEARCH AND ACCUMULATE DATA
Participants must locate relevant, supportable, factual data to justify their pro or con stand on the issue.

SELECT AND ORGANIZE
Participants must prioritize the information located and rank the information from most important and useable to the least.

DETERMINE THE TWO STRONGEST
Participants must identify, formulate and practice the strongest statements possible supporting their position on the issue.

SIDE ASSIGNED
Assigning a side is usually reserved for more advanced debaters and is done by the moderator.

PRO OPENING STATEMENT
The debater supporting the issue makes the most significant and substantive argument possible for his or her stand.

CON OPENING STATEMENT
The debater opposing the issue makes the most significant and substantive argument possible for his or her stand.

FIRST "PRO" ARGUMENT
The debater supporting the issue expands his or her position using supportive data gathered in research.

FIRST "CON" ARGUMENT
The debater opposing the issue expands his or her position using supportive data gathered in research.

SECOND "PRO" ARGUMENT
The debater supporting the issue further expands his or her position using supportive data gathered in research.

SECOND "CON" ARGUMENT
The debater opposing the issue further expands his or her position using supportive data gathered in research.

FIRST "CON" REBUTTAL
The debater opposing the issue presents a civilized disagreement in which points are made and supported to refute or contradict the points made by the PRO arguments and statements.

FIRST "PRO" REBUTTAL
The debater supporting the issue presents a civilized disagreement in which points are made and supported to refute or contradict the points made by the CON arguments and statements.

SECOND "CON" REBUTTAL
The debater opposing the issue presents a civilized disagreement in which additional points are made and supported to refute or contradict the points made by the PRO arguments and statements.

SECOND "PRO" REBUTTAL
The debater supporting the issue presents a civilized disagreement in which additional points are made and supported to refute or contradict the points made by the CON arguments and statements.

"PRO" CLOSING STATEMENT
The debater supporting the issue is given the opportunity to summarize and justify the rationale for PRO position on the issue.

"CON" CLOSING STATEMENT
The debater opposing the issue is given the opportunity to summarize and justify the rationale for CON position on the issue.

JUDGMENT/EVALUATION
Based on the debaters' performance, use of supporting data and accuracy, a winner is determined.

RESEARCH FOR DEBATE TOPIC

You may choose to record your research on this page.

DEBATE TOPIC: _____

_____

_____

_____

_____

_____

_____

_____

_____

_____

_____

_____

_____

_____

_____

_____

_____

_____

_____

_____

_____

_____

_____

_____

_____

YES and NO!
(FOR OR AGAINST)
Part 1

Record the data you have accumulated from your research regarding both sides the debate topic prior to knowing which side of issue will be your responsibility.

DEBATE TOPIC:

_____

YES (FOR)	NO (AGAINST)

YES and NO!
(FOR OR AGAINST)
Part 2

Based on all of your research, choose and record the strongest arguments supporting each stand on the issue. Refer to your research data base as needed.

DEBATE TOPIC:

_____

YES (FOR)	NO (AGAINST)

YES and NO!
(FOR OR AGAINST)
Part 3

**Here are two options, the choice of which should be made
PRIOR to selecting an issue to debate!**

1. The moderator can randomly assign
a side for the issue. This means that
you should be equally prepared
to take either point of view
on the issue.

2. The opposing teams or individual
participants may have pre-selected their
stand and agreed on their positions
regarding the issue at hand.
This method allows for more directed
and focused preparation,
especially for those new to
the debating process.

YES and NO!
(FOR OR AGAINST)
Part 4

YES - FOR

Determine the two strongest arguments for your position on the issue and rehearse in preparation for the debate. Information from the FOR and AGAINST sides of the issue may be useful as negations for the opposite point of view.

DEBATE TOPIC:

_____

ARGUMENT #1

_____
_____
_____
_____
_____
_____

ARGUMENT #2

_____
_____
_____
_____
_____
_____

YES and NO!
(FOR OR AGAINST)
Part 4

NO - AGAINST

Determine the two strongest arguments for your position on the issue and rehearse in preparation for the debate. Information from the FOR and AGAINST sides of the issue may be useful as negations for the opposite point of view.

DEBATE TOPIC:

_____

ARGUMENT #1

_____
_____
_____
_____
_____
_____

ARGUMENT #2

_____
_____
_____
_____
_____
_____

MY PLANNING SHEETS
YES - FOR

You know the debatable issue, have completed your research, have determined the strongest arguments, and have been assigned to or selected a specific stand. Now it is time to get ready for the debate. Use the following pages to plan and prepare what you will say during the debate. Remember to use the DEBATE CHECKLIST!

OPENING STATEMENT

_____
_____
_____
_____
_____
_____
_____
_____

FIRST ARGUMENT

_____
_____
_____
_____

SECOND ARGUMENT

_____
_____
_____
_____

FIRST REBUTTAL: Based on the Opposition's Argument(s)

_____

_____

_____

_____

_____

SECOND REBUTTAL: Based on the Opposition's Argument(s)

_____

_____

_____

_____

_____

CLOSING STATEMENT
Make the strongest possible summation supporting your position on the issue.

_____

_____

_____

_____

_____

_____

_____

_____

_____

_____

_____

_____

MY PLANNING SHEETS
NO - AGAINST

You know the debatable issue, have completed your research, have determined the strongest arguments, and have been assigned to or selected a specific stand. Now it is time to get ready for the debate. Use the following pages to plan and prepare what you will say during the debate. Remember to use the DEBATE CHECKLIST!

OPENING STATEMENT

_____

_____

_____

_____

_____

_____

_____

_____

FIRST ARGUMENT

_____

_____

_____

_____

SECOND ARGUMENT

_____

_____

_____

_____

FIRST REBUTTAL: Based on the Opposition's Argument(s)

_____
_____
_____
_____
_____
_____

SECOND REBUTTAL: Based on the Opposition's Argument(s)

_____
_____
_____
_____
_____
_____

CLOSING STATEMENT
Make the strongest possible summation supporting your position on the issue.

_____
_____
_____
_____
_____
_____
_____
_____
_____
_____
_____
_____

DEBATE TOPICS

BE IT RESOLVED!

A list of "issues"—matters that can have differing points of view, stands or sides—is provided. The list is divided into categories and reflects an interdisciplinary approach towards topics from an array of discipline fields. An interdisciplinary approach integrates thinking and learning skills and unifies content and process. You may choose to use the issues provided, create your own topics based upon your curriculum, or use the student-made Create Your Own! activity issues.

ENGLISH/LANGUAGE ARTS

Comic books are literature.

The novel on the printed page is dead.

Hip hop is poetry.

There are only five plot lines.

All students should study Shakespeare.

Parsing sentences is worthwhile.

Computers make handwriting obsolete.

Comics & illustrated novels should not be used in reading classes.

All of the great novels have been written.

Print media should be discontinued in favor of electronic media.

SCIENCE-1

Global warming is a myth.

The U.S. should invest in space exploration.

Nuclear energy is too dangerous.

We are alone in the universe.

Neither nature nor nurture determines personality traits.

Cloning is the way of the future.

Sports drinks are beneficial.

The human little toe is unnecessary.

Yawning is contagious.

There are no more elements for the Periodic Table.

SCIENCE-2

Every person in the world is responsible for changes in the natural environment.

The U.S. must expand exploration of the seas' resources.

The World Health Organization must have power over any country in terms of stopping medical outbreaks of disease.

Alternative fuels should not be developed from food sources.

There is intelligent life on other planets.

Neither plants nor animals are more important to a balanced earth ecology.

Water is not the world's most important natural resource.

NASA and the U.S. government must limit future exploration to an unmanned space program.

The U.S. government must turn space exploration over to private industry.

What we perceive as the solar system, the Milky Way, and the universe are really an atom, a molecule and an object in a larger world.

SOCIAL STUDIES-1

Slavery was unique to pre-Civil War America.

China is the next major world power.

The popular vote should be the determiner of the U.S. presidential election.

The only major ancient civilizations were those that surrounded the Mediterranean.

Machiavelli was right.

The federal government must not regulate education.

The U.S. should have dropped the atomic bomb in WW II.

Economics had nothing to do with the fall of the Soviet Union.

National boundaries are never permanent.

A country should use a boycott of a "sports event," such as the Olympics, to change human-rights behaviors.

SOCIAL STUDIES-2

Capital punishment for crimes should not be part of the legal system of the United States.

U.S. Supreme Court justices should continue to be appointed for life.

It is time to rethink and modify the five top priorities of the United Nations.

There was no long-term significance to any year or decade in the Middle Ages.

The U.S. Free Trade Agreement is a positive economic step for the country.

Great Britain's parliamentary form of government is superior to the democratic form of government of the United States.

There should be no constitutional limitations on the number of years for a U.S. presidential term.

Public transportation and mass transit will never be the primary means of commuting in the United States.

The world is ready for one, universal language for use in world politics and international commerce.

The United States must be bilingual.

MATH

Metric must be the global measurement norm.

All students should master algebra.

Math is essential to all aspects of life.

Pi must have an end.

Math is a science.

The binary system is the One.

The Industrial Military Complex, first described by former U.S. President Dwight D. Eisenhower, rules world economics.

There must be one global currency.

Algebra is not essential for life.

The metric system is superior to the English measurement system.

THE ARTS

Advertising is art.
Modern art is not trash.
Ballet dancers are athletes.
Computer generated graphics is art.
The federal government must support the arts.
European classical music is the best.
Musical theater is trite.
Artists should be paid when their work appears on the Internet.
There is every reason why a successful athlete should become a media star.
All cultures and civilizations produce art.

ETHICS-1

Honesty is not a virtue.

The Internet should not be censored.

Old people should be kept together in one housing facility.

China's one-child policy is appropriate.

Table manners are old fashioned.

Religion is always a force for peace.

Human cloning is acceptable.

Self-regulation by industry is the most effective method for oversight of their actions and practices.

Students should go on some sort of non-violent "strike" if their school does not meet their academic and human-rights needs.

Professional athletes and media stars should not be held accountable as role models.

ETHICS-2

Poverty can be eradicated by charitable and support organizations issuing "microcredit" to the impoverished.

A community service draft should be an alternative to the universal military draft in the United States.

A prisoner on "death row" should receive "state of the art" medical treatment if...

Downloading of information from the Internet should not be subject to copyright laws.

Personal safety is more important than personal liberties and independence in these dangerous times.

Athletes and media stars are icons who deserve multi-million dollar salaries.

Wars are won by the most deserving side.

Honesty is relative.

Personal success is not measured by income.

All students should pass algebra, be in a school play, and be on a varsity team to graduate from high school.

SOCIOLOGY

Video games do not cause crime.

Cities are superior places to raise children.

The nuclear family is dead.

All cultures can reach the same level of sophistication.

Computers must replace teachers.

Social groups do not determine behavior.

Teachers' salary should be based entirely on the success levels of their students' academic performance.

State universities are better than private ones.

A universal military draft is necessary in the United States.

Children should be free to and encouraged to create their own ideas of "play."

PERSONAL-1

Children do not need to listen to their parents.

Bullying is a natural part of growing up.

The driving age should not be lowered.

School uniforms are a good thing.

Chores develop character.

Gossip is great.

Rumors rule.

Homework helps students learn.

Uniforms should be mandatory in U.S. public schools.

Homework should be part of the overall grade in a subject area.

PERSONAL-2

Grades should be based less upon "work produced" than on knowledge about a subject area.

Comic books should be used in reading classes.

Dogs are the best possible family pet.

Cell phones do not belong in public schools.

Cell-phone use while driving should not be against the law.

America should have a new number #1 sport every year.

Public schools in the United States should be in continuous session, year round.

Children should always defer to their elders.

Bed time should be determined by the person going to bed.

Students should be grouped by ability in school classes.

CREATE YOUR OWN!

You have had the experience of taking part in debate(s). It is now time for you to have the opportunity to create debate topics that are of interest to you. You may use one or more of the "Be It Resolved!" categories listed and/or come up with your own categories. Once you have a list, share it with your teacher and your classmates as possibilities for upcoming debate topic ideas.

BE IT RESOLVED...!

ENGLISH/LANGUAGE ARTS

_____
_____
_____
_____
_____
_____
_____
_____

SCIENCE

_____
_____
_____
_____
_____
_____
_____
_____
_____
_____
_____

SOCIAL STUDIES

_____
_____
_____
_____
_____
_____
_____
_____
_____

MATH

_____
_____
_____
_____
_____
_____

THE ARTS

_____
_____
_____
_____
_____
_____
_____
_____

ETHICS

_____
_____
_____
_____
_____
_____
_____
_____
_____
_____
_____

SOCIOLOGY

_____
_____
_____
_____
_____
_____
_____

PERSONAL

_____
_____
_____
_____
_____
_____

NEW CATEGORY
(OR CONTINUATION OF ANOTHER CATEGORY)

CATEGORY: _____

_____

_____

_____

_____

_____

_____

_____

CATEGORY: _____

_____

_____

_____

_____

_____

_____

_____

_____

_____

CATEGORY: _____

_____

_____

_____

_____

_____

_____

_____

_____

_____

REFERENCES

42eXplore. Retrieved February 6, 2008, from http://42explore.com/debate.htm

About.com: inline skating. Retrieved June 24, 2008, from http://inlineskating.about.com

Bloom, Benjamin S. & David R. Krathwohl. *Taxonomy of Educational Objectives: The Classification of Educational Goals by a Committee of College and University Examiners. Handbook 1: Cognitive domain.* New York , Longmans, 1956.

Education World. Retrieved February 6, 2008, from http://www.education-world.com. (Debate).

FreeDictionary.com, The. Farlex, Inc. Retrieved March 13, 2008, from http://www.thefreedictionary.com/Dictionary.htm

McAlpine, Jim., Betty Weincek, Sue Jeweler, and Marion Finkbinder. *Investigating Earth Science.* Hawthorne, NJ: Educational Impressions, Inc., 2003.

Merriam-Webster Online. Retrieved April, May, June, 2008, from http://www.merriam-webster.com

Tiddlywinks: Simplified Rules of Tiddlywinks. Retrieved July 6, 2008, from http://www.tiddlywinks.org

Tucker's Tiddlywinks: North American Tiddlywinks Association. Retrieved June 24, 2008, from http://www.tiddlywinks.org

What makes a sport 'Olympic'? Retrieved July 9, 2008, from http://encarta.msn.com

WikiAnswers - What criteria does a sport have to meet to be an Olympic sport. Retrieved July 9, 2008, from http://wiki.answers.com

Wikipedia, the Free Encyclopedia. Wikimedia Foundation. Retrieved March 13, 2008, from http://enwikipedia.org. (Debate)

<u>Notes</u>